T0271768

# More Fun Games and Activities
# for Children with Dyslexia

# More Fun Games and Activities for Children with Dyslexia

## How to Learn Smarter with a Dyslexic Brain

### Alais Winton

Illustrated by Hannah Millard

**Jessica Kingsley Publishers**
London and Philadelphia

First published in Great Britain in 2022 by Jessica Kingsley Publishers
An imprint of Hodder & Stoughton Ltd
An Hachette Company

1

The fonts, layout and overall design of this book have been prepared
according to dyslexia-friendly principles. At JKP we aim to make our
books' content accessible to as many readers as possible.

A CIP catalogue record for this title is available from the
British Library and the Library of Congress

ISBN 978 1 78775 447 8
eISBN 978 1 78775 448 5

Printed and bound in Great Britain by TJ Books Limited

Jessica Kingsley Publishers' policy is to use papers that are natural,
renewable and recyclable products and made from wood grown in
sustainable forests. The logging and manufacturing processes are expected
to conform to the environmental regulations of the country of origin.

Jessica Kingsley Publishers
Carmelite House
50 Victoria Embankment
London EC4Y 0DZ

www.jkp.com

For anyone who finds learning a
challenge – you got this!

For anyone who has helped me learn – thank you.

# Contents

# Acknowledgements

Thank you to Hannah Millard for amazing illustrations and coming on board late on in this process.

You have a real gift.

As always, a huge thank you to Hannah Rackham, for being my 'bestie', always being so encouraging about my work in dyslexia and reminding me why it's important to keep doing it.

A big thank you to Simon Green, for saving what I had already written of this book, installing a new hard drive and setting up my computer again so I could finish this book. I probably owe you more chocolate.

Thanks to Amy Lankester-Owen, my editor, for ongoing support and always finding time to talk to me despite our busy schedules.

Thank you to Hannah Snetsinger and everyone at Jessica Kingsley who has been involved with the production of this book.

Thank you to Jack Churchill for input and updates on the C-PEN® ReaderPen™, and for the work you do to support dyslexic learners.

A massive thank you to all the young dyslexics I work with (or have worked with) and your families. All the games and activities in this book were played or carried out with you first and your honest feedback and progress in learning is what determines what is included in my book.

To Morgan Lewis for all your hard work, honest opinions and making such epic progress in reading – keep it up!

Thank you to my work colleagues, especially Isabel, Sara, Vicky and Emily B. who keep me smiling and reasonably sane.

Thank you to Rhys for teaching me how to use a pole lathe, which was the most fun I have had for a while.

Finally, thank you to anyone else who helped and supported me with the writing of this book.

**CHAPTER 1**

# Hello Again

My name is Alais (pronounced Alice) and I am dyslexic.

Being dyslexic can mean different things to different people, but it usually means that spelling and reading can be very tricky.

The good thing about being dyslexic is that it can mean that you are very creative and can think in pictures instead of words.

A few years ago I wrote a book about games and activities for dyslexic children.

This is the same kind of book, but you don't need to have read the first book to enjoy this one or play the games in it.

I had a phone call last month with a mum (of a dyslexic child) who had contacted me.

The mum I spoke to had played the games in the first book with her daughter and was keen for more ideas and games they might enjoy.

She also wanted more games to help her daughter overcome her challenges in learning.

I work with dyslexic children and teenagers, helping them with anything that they find hard.

As human beings we enjoy doing things we like – the same things we were good at to begin with.

We stay away from things we don't like, things we may have found difficult to start with, so fun and enjoyment matter when it comes to learning.

Choose the games in this book that are the most fun for you as you will want to learn the most from those.

If you have ideas about how you would like to add to the games or invent your own, go for it!

You might think of something while you are playing the game or doing the activity, or you may think of something later on.

I play these games with the dyslexic students I work with and hope that you like them. I hope that you will find them fun but also learn something.

I have been a teacher for a long time and have spent a lot of time thinking about how I learn best.

I learn best using pictures, images and movement. I don't learn well using reading and writing like some of my non-dyslexic friends do.

Some dyslexics might learn best using pictures or movement like me, or they might learn better using music or teamwork.

It is a very good idea to find out how you learn best – your learning strength. I have included a quiz in Chapter 2 to help you find out how you learn best.

If you learn best using pictures, you are likely to get the most out of the 'I Like to See It' games in this book.

If you learn best using movement, you are likely to get the most out of the 'I Like to Move It' games in this book.

If you like playing with friends or family then

working together might be your thing. Lots of the games in this book need two or more players.

However, we are all different, so you don't have to stick to one thing. You can try all the games and find the ones you like the most. Many of the games, playing cards and answer sheets are marked with the symbol ✳ and are downloadable at www.jkp.com/catalogue/book/9781787754478.

Please remember that whatever result you get in the quiz your strength may change over time.

Also, you may get a high score in more than one thing; this is great news as it means you have strengths in different things, so you can pick whatever you enjoy more.

# CHAPTER 2

# How Do You Like to Learn?

People think in different ways because we don't all have the same kind of brain.

This means that people also learn in different ways.

Most subjects in school (apart from Art and Drama) have a teacher standing at the front of the class explaining what is on the board and the children write notes.

For many people, especially those who are dyslexic, this method does not work very well.

If your English and Maths lessons are not normally

like this, you probably have a super smart teacher who might also be a bit of a rebel – lucky you!

But if sitting and writing notes sounds like the classes at your school, and it doesn't work well for you, take the following quiz to find out what is your best way to learn.

Many of the best ways to learn are by using the senses, for example what you can see, hear and touch or move. You might also learn well by working with other people.

You may get a high score in more than one part of the quiz; this will just mean that you can 'mix and match' and choose which method you want to use.

# How you like to learn quiz

## Is it true for you?

Read the statements on each of the sheets that follow and decide whether they are true for you, answering 'yes', 'maybe' and 'no'. Score 1 point for 'yes', half a point for 'maybe' and no points for 'no'. Add up the totals for each section and see which method works best for you.

# Visual-Spatial (picture thinker)

◯ You think of an image or picture when someone says a word, not the letters that make up the word.

◯ You often find yourself doodling when you are making notes or feeling bored.

◯ You find it easier to understand something new if there is a diagram, picture or YouTube video to explain it.

◯ You prefer games which use visual skills, for example Pictionary™, Qwirkle™, Pairs or a games console.

◯ You enjoy watching films and TV programmes.

# Physical (movement thinker)

◯ You enjoy PE and/or practical and active lessons at school.

◯ You have been described as a practical or 'hands on' person.

◯ You find it difficult to sit still in class, or other people have described you as a fidget.

◯ You take part in a sport or exercise outside of school time.

◯ If you are learning something new, you prefer to do this in an active way, rather than read a book or follow written or verbal instructions.

## Musical (music thinker)

○ You listen to music on your MP3 player, Spotify® or a smartphone whenever you can.

○ You wouldn't want to think about a world without music.

○ You play an instrument or sing.

○ You often find yourself thinking of music from TV programmes or adverts.

○ When you learn something new you like to listen to instructions rather than read them.

# Interpersonal (team thinker)

○ You enjoy games played as a team, for example multi-player console games, board games, tag.

○ Other people come to you to ask for advice.

○ You are good at talking to people and sorting out any arguments.

○ You are outgoing and would rather be out with friends than at home alone.

○ When you learn something new you like to 'figure it out' as part of a team.

(Adapted from Gardner 2006)

Make a note of which aspect your highest score was in.

You could try activities and games from all the following chapters but the one about your strongest sense will usually work best for you.

# CHAPTER 3

# Let's Work Together

Teamwork is very important in learning. It means that we can put our different strengths together – we can share what we already know but also learn from what someone else knows.

The following games can be played with friends or family.

The first game helps improve reading and spelling, which can be an everyday challenge for someone who is dyslexic.

It also aims to help improve use of past tense words. Many of my dyslexic learners think that to change a word to something that happened in the past you just add <u>ed</u> to the word.

Although this is true for some words, for example **jump** to **jumped**, **walk** to **walked** and so on, it is not true for all words. Examples which do not add <u>ed</u> include: **wear** to **wore**, **throw** to **threw** and **sing** to **sang**. This game will help with the ones that change and don't just add <u>ed</u>.

# ▶ STAR GAME

*For two to four players.*

## You will need

- *an old Scrabble™ board or piece of card with a grid of squares and a star in the centre square like a Scrabble™ board*

- *playing pieces or counters — you could use small buttons, pieces you already have or tiddlywinks counters*

- *a die (just one dice)*

- *playing cards (for examples see page 128, but you can also make your own)*

- *answer sheet (example included on page 132).*

# How to play

You may want to ask an adult for help setting up this activity.

Place one pile of cards in each of the four corners of the board:

- ▸ past tense cards

- ▸ spelling cards

- ▸ reading cards

- ▸ random — a mix of all three categories.

Each player selects a start position at the edge of the board.

Choose a player to begin. This could be the youngest or whoever rolls the highest number on the die.

Player one then rolls the die and moves towards one of the piles of playing cards.

Players take it in turns to reach the playing cards.

Once a player is on a square next to the cards they take a card from the top of the pile and answer the question or complete the task.

If this is done correctly the player 'wins' and collects the card.

If this is incorrect the player puts the card on the bottom of the pile, waits for their next turn and then takes the new card at the top of the pile and answers that.

When a player has collected four cards (one from each pile) they move to the middle square with the star and shout 'I am a star!' The first player to do this is the winner.

# ▶ VERB SUPER SCORE

For two or more players.

What Cameron thought about this game:

> 'This game is good because it expands your vocabulary. It is fun because it's competitive. I was good at choosing the best categories for my cards.' (Cameron Jenkins, age 12)

## You will need

- playing cards (see page 133 for examples)

- playing cards template to create your own cards (see page 138).

## How to play

You may want to ask an adult for help setting up this activity.

Deal the cards. Player one looks at their top card only. They select a category, e.g. 'Power', and read it out loud with the points for this category.

The second player looks at their top card and

compares the score for the category. If their score is lower, they pass their card to player one; if it is higher they keep both cards.

Whichever player wins selects the next category.

The overall winner is the player who has collected the most cards when one player has no cards left.

The next game is included as a result of a real-life problem.

My student, who was 11 at the time, was given a test in his English class to write an extract from a Shakespeare play in 'modern' English.

In other words, he had to look at the language of Shakespeare, which is old and different, and try to decide what this would mean today.

My student was very confused and felt like he had done very badly in this test.

This is why I have used words often used by Shakespeare in this game of pairs, in case you get the same kind of test.

I am including an answer sheet but try to guess as many as you can before looking at the answers.

#  SHAKESPEARE PAIRS

*For two to four players.*

## You will need

- *pairs word cards (make these using the examples on page 141 from card of one colour — extras can be made by an adult or just ask them for help).*

## How to play

Once you have made all the cards, mix them up and put them face down on the floor or on a table.

Then turn over two cards at a time. If you match

the right Shakespearian word with what the word means today, you have won a pair and can keep both cards.

If the cards do not match, turn them face down in the same place and then either try again (if it is just you playing) or the next player has a turn.

If you do win a pair then you get another go before the next player takes their turn.

At the end of the game each player counts the number of pairs they have to see who has won.

# CHAPTER 4

# I Like to Move It

If you like to learn through movement then you may enjoy the games in this chapter.

It can be hard to know when to use a comma, especially if you are dyslexic.

I was told at school to use commas in my writing when I needed to take a breath.

The problem with this is that I can talk for ages without taking a breath.

This meant that I used to write very, very long sentences without any commas.

Some of the young people I work with think that commas are boring and don't matter.

I have learnt that the humble comma can be really important – it could even save a life.

Think about the following two sentences:

1. Let's eat, grandma.

2. Let's eat grandma.

The first sentence means that you would like to have food with grandma.

The second sentence means that grandma is the food you want to eat!

So now you know how important commas can be, the next game will help you to learn how best to use them.

#  WHERE'S MY COMMA?

*For two or more players.*

## You will need

- *a list of sentences with commas (see page 37 for some examples).*

## How to play

You may want to ask an adult for help setting up this activity.

One player in the game can see the examples with punctuation (adult or child) and the other player/s guess where the punctuation goes using a sound and movement to represent a comma. You may want to use a large paintbrush or wand if you have one.

One of my learners made a sweeping move with their hand and chose the sound 'oh no not a comma'.

This sound does not need to be a sentence or phrase. It could be a sigh, a yawn or a meow, for example.

Here are the rules for using commas.

Commas can be used to:

- separate items in a list

- surround extra information

- break up a long sentence.

The word **and** usually replaces a comma.

Player one reads the first example sentence out loud.

Player two listens.

Player one reads the sentence again and this time player two puts in their sound and movement where they think there should be a comma.

Were they correct? If not repeat the sentence.

If it was correct player two makes up their own sentence and player one creates a sound and movement where they think there should be a comma.

Repeat this stage with example sentence number two and then example sentence number three.

After each round, or at the end of the game, the players can make up their own example showing that particular use of the comma (written or verbally), and an adult can check the punctuation is correct. For instance, if the comma is used in a list, they could make up a list of football players they like.

## Example sentences for 'Where's my comma?' game

In a list:

My favourite sandwich would have: bacon, lettuce, tomato, onion and mayonnaise.

Extra information:

My sister, who is a nurse, will know how to bandage your arm.

To break up a sentence:

Rugby practice may be cancelled this week, so make sure you check the notice board.

Other examples of sentences using commas can be found at Twinkl and BBC Bitesize (see Resources).

The next game is aimed at making reading more fun.

# ▶ DARTS WORD HUNT

*For two to four players.*

## You will need

- ▸ word cards: these could use words taken from a school list, could be made by parents or adults or they could be bought (see Resources)

- ▸ a children's dart board

- ▸ velcro darts or balls.

## How to play

*Put a number on each word card. If you are using two darts start with the lowest number that two darts could score. On my board this is 20 (10 + 10).*

*Hide the word cards around the room you are in, number side up.*

Player one throws their dart/s at the board and then finds the card with the number on which matches their score.

The player must then read out loud the word on the card.

If the word is correct they keep the card; if not they find a new hiding place for it.

The next player does the same as player one.

If a player scores the number of a card that has already been collected they miss a go and wait for their next turn.

Players take turns until all the word cards have been collected by the players.

Whoever has the most cards at the end is the winner.

If players of different ages or reading ability are playing together you could include different words on each card.

For example, you could have a card with:

A: Hat          B: Turn          C: Invention

*The player who reads A finds reading very hard.*

*The player who reads B finds some words hard.*

*The player who reads C is a very good reader.*

*Players can change their letter (level of difficulty) over time.*

> 'Playing darts and finding words made this fun. I learnt how to read new words by playing this game.' (Cameron, dyslexic learner)

Some letter combinations make the same sound, and it can be tricky to know which one to use in different words.

For example:

- ay

- ei

- -a-e

all make an A sound.

This game can be a good way to learn which letter combination to use if movement is your thing.

## ▶ DROP THE BALL

*For two to four players.*

### You will *need*

- ▸ *three or four A4 size cards*

- ▸ *a list of words containing ay, ei, or -a-e (see the Spellzone website in Resources)*

- ▸ *a bold pen, for example permanent marker pen*

- ▸ *a small soft ball.*

## How to play

You may want to ask an adult for help setting up this activity.

Write three or four letter combinations on A4 size card, one combination on each sheet of card.

Place your card sheets on the floor, making sure that they don't overlap.

One player will read the first word on the list out loud.

Player two must drop the ball onto the letter combination that they think is correct for that word, for example **ay** for the word **say**.

If there are only two players they then swap over.

If there are more than two players each player takes turns at reading or guessing where to drop the ball.

Each correct ball drop scores a point and the player with the most points at the end is the winner.

# ▶ ACTING OUT

For two or more players.

## You will need

- two sheets of paper

- pens

- *scissors*

- *a list of verbs*

- *a list of adverbs.*

## How to play

*Verbs are doing words.*

*Example list of verbs:*

| | | |
|---|---|---|
| - *run* | - *dance* | - *eat* |
| - *walk* | - *climb* | - *fight* |
| - *sing* | - *fly* | - *dress* |

*Adverbs are how, when, where or why you do something.*

*Example list of adverbs:*

| | |
|---|---|
| - *quickly* | - *recklessly* |
| - *slowly* | - *confidently* |
| - *grumpily* | - *shyly* |
| - *happily* | - *tiredly* |
| - *carefully* | - *energetically* |

On the first piece of paper write a list of verbs. You can use my examples or make up your own.

Cut out each word and fold the paper.

On the second sheet of paper write a list of adverbs. You can use my examples or make up your own.

Cut out each word and fold the paper.

You can use two different colours of paper if it helps — one for verbs and the other for adverbs. Place the folded pieces of paper in two separate piles.

The first player chooses two folded pieces of paper: one verb and one adverb.

The first player then acts out the verb in the style of the adverb.

For example, the verb might be **run** and the adverb might be **slowly.**

So the first player acts out running slowly and the other players must guess the two words chosen.

When the players have guessed correctly the

next player chooses two words (one verb and one adverb) and acts out the words.

You can do this as a group just for fun.

If you want to score points you can play in teams, one actor and one guesser, and give points for the most correct guesses or quickest correct guess.

Remember you might get some odd combos. For example, you could have **fight tiredly** or **eat carefully**.

You will need to use your best acting skills for those.

# CHAPTER 5

# I Like to See It

The first activity is based on a card game that you may have heard of called Happy Families.

The aim of the game is very simple: you are trying to collect a whole family of each set.

In this version, instead of using jobs (e.g. Mrs Bun the Baker), pictures and words are used.

# ▶ HAPPY FAMILIES WITH PICTURE CARDS

*For two to four players.*

*You can buy picture cards (see the 'Stuff to buy' list in Resources) or you can make your own. You could also check out printable resources online (see the Twinkl website in Resources). To make your own follow the instructions below.*

## You will **need**

- *two sheets of card*
- *coloured pens or pencils*
- *scissors*
- *a pencil*
- *a ruler.*

*Using the pencil and the ruler, divide each of your card sheets into twelve sections. This will give you 24 cards in total. Make sure they are the same size.*

*Cut out the sections to make 24 cards. Decide on your six groups of words — for example, farm* animals, minibeasts, vegetables, fruits, transport and clothes — and draw a picture on one side of each card for each group. Make sure you have four cards in each group so you end up with six groups.

Ask someone to write the words for the pictures you have drawn on the other side of the cards.

## How to play

Deal all the cards and decide who will take the first turn.

The player who is holding the cards can see their pictures, so they know what they have in their hand. The other players can see the back of the cards (the words) so must read the word to ask for a card from another player.

They will ask another player for a card, so they could say 'Have you got a cat?' If the second player has a cat they then give it to the first.

Player one then asks for another card.

If player one gets a word wrong or can't remember it the players swap over and player two asks for cards one at a time, and so on.

*The goal is to collect as many full groups as you can.*

*If you collect all the cards in that group place them face up on the table in front of you.*

*The game is over when the players aren't holding any cards.*

*The winner is the player who collects the most groups.*

---

Some dyslexic learners find word searches very hard, but if you are a visual learner you will enjoy the following activity even if it takes a bit of time to crack it.

# ▶ SILENT LETTER WORD SEARCH

Find the words at the bottom in this table.
Remember that words can go up, down, diagonally
or backwards.

| W | G | N | D | R | A | K | G | W | T |
|---|---|---|---|---|---|---|---|---|---|
| R | B | E | R | E | N | M | N | H | S |
| E | E | H | O | O | S | T | G | E | R |
| B | L | W | W | E | T | I | R | W | E |
| M | B | T | S | I | R | W | G | L | K |
| U | E | M | O | N | G | H | P | N | N |
| L | M | P | A | G | A | A | O | R | E |
| P | B | M | I | L | C | T | E | H | W |

| | | |
|---|---|---|
| PLUMBER | TWO | KNEE |
| DESIGN | KNOT | ANSWER |
| WHEN | WHAT | CLIMB |
| SWORD | WRITE | LAMB |
| GNOME | RIGHT | |
| WRIST | KNOW | |

# ▶ CRAFT CLASH: SPELLING SIGNS

## You will need

- A3 size paper

- coloured pens

- coloured pencils

- paints

- a paintbrush

- glitter

- fun stickers.

## How to play

You might like to ask an adult for help setting up this activity.

Choose a list of words with a similar spelling pattern, such as: **light, sight, might**. Also put in one or two words that sound the same but are spelt differently. For this list you could pick **white**.

Make sure you have the right spelling for each word — you could ask someone to print out a list.

Using the paints, pens and pencils write your words on the A3 paper.

The words do not have to be in a straight line. They can be curvy and written in any direction.

Fill the paper with your words using a mixture of paint, pens and coloured pencils, for the same word if you want to.

For example, write your word: **light**, with one letter (l) in pen, two letters (ig) in paint and two letters (ht) in coloured pencil.

Then decorate your words using glitter, stickers and any other craft items.

You could add flowers or hearts to your words. As long as you can still see the letters you can go wild!

When it is dry put your new sign somewhere you can see it every day.

If you keep looking at it, after a little while you will remember how to spell these words.

When you are sure you can spell all the words on your sign you could make a new one with different words.

# ▶ WORD BINGO

For two or more players.

## You will need

- bingo cards (one per player)

- a pencil

- a pen

- a ruler

- counters

- a small prize

- paper.

## How to play

Each player needs to choose a group of twelve words, maybe words that are difficult to read.

I often use 'sight' words. These are words that do not have a picture you could think of to help you remember the meaning. The word **rabbit** can be tricky to spell but when you read it you can think of a rabbit to help you remember it.

'Sight' word examples:

| | | |
|---|---|---|
| if | our | what |
| that | then | why |
| these | when | or |
| those | who | even |
| of | where | are |

Using the pencil and the ruler, draw six squares on your bingo cards. Write the words, one word in each square. This will make two bingo cards. For more cards you will need more words. You can ask someone to help or do this bit for you.

Write all the words on the cards on pieces of paper, fold them up and put them in a pot.

Take it in turns to pull out a piece of paper, read the word and cover it with a counter if it is on your card.

Then refold the paper and put it back in the pot.

The winner is the person who covers all their squares first and shouts 'house' or 'bingo'.

If you don't have time to make this you can buy a readymade version of 'sight' words bingo (see Resources).

It can be hard to know which way round the letters **ei** and **ie** are in words.

There is a well-known rule: 'I before E except after C'. This means that unless the letter **c** comes before these letters in a word the order is **ie**. So in f**ie**ld and sh**ie**ld the order is **ie**.

If there is a **c** then the order is reversed, so in rec**ei**ve and c**ei**ling the order is **ei**.

The English language can be very tricky so there are of course some words that break this rule. This game will help you to learn the rule breakers.

## ▶ EI/IE MAZE

*For two players.*

### You will need

- ‣ *a maze — you could draw your own or print the one in this book*

- ‣ *a clues page*

- ‣ *an answer page*

- ‣ *a clean paintbrush.*

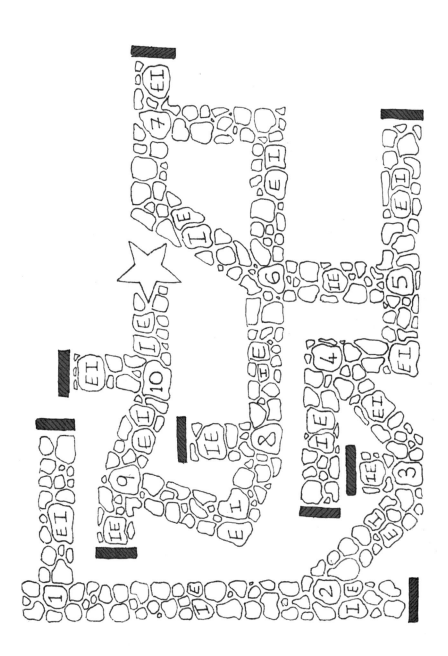

*Example **ei** or **ie** maze clues:*

1. The study of biology, chemistry, physics or all three

2. How heavy something is

3. Person who lives next door

4. How Santa travels

5. Think it is true

6. Wooden object used for protection

7. Very old

8. Number after seven

9. Strange

10. From another planet

*Example **ei** or **ie** maze answers:*

| | |
|---|---|
| 1. sci**e**nce | 4. sl**eig**h |
| 2. w**eig**ht | 5. bel**ie**ve |
| 3. n**eig**hbour | 6. sh**ie**ld |

7. anc**ie**nt

9. w**ei**rd

8. **ei**ght

10. al**ie**n

## How to play

Player one will give player two the first clue.

The second player must guess the correct word and then decide if the word has an **ei** or **ie**.

Whichever order they choose they should follow the letter they have chosen using the paintbrush to follow the route.

If player two is correct it will take them to the next clue.

If the player is not correct it will take them to a dead end.

The game is complete when player two reaches the centre of the maze.

Be warned! I have added a tricky bit in mine which looks right to begin with but leads to another dead end.

When player two reaches the centre of the maze

you can swap over and player one can choose the letter combination for each word.

The winner is the player who gets to the centre the fastest.

You could use the maze again with different words but the same **ei/ie** combinations.

For example, answer 1 is **ie** after a **c** combo (which is a rule breaker) so other words you could use might be:

- ▸ vacancies

- ▸ fancied

- ▸ species

- ▸ policies

You could also keep the same words but swap the order as long as they still match **ei/ie** for each answer.

Good luck! I'm sure you will learn those pesky rule breakers in no time.

# CHAPTER 6

# I Like to Hear It

Most people with dyslexia will spell words how they sound.

English words can be tricky, so this way of spelling in many cases does not work.

This game is aimed at learning sounds that letters or letter combinations make.

One very clever child I worked with thought that the word **tree** started with <u>ch</u> making it hard to spell and almost everyone I work with thinks that **cute** starts with the letter <u>q</u>.

I agree that qute makes more sense, but we are stuck with cute.

# ▶ SOMETHING BEGINNING WITH...

For two or more players.

## You will need

- cardboard

- pens

- scissors

- a ruler

- a pencil

- a timer.

Using the pencil and the ruler, draw 12 squares, the same size, on a piece of card.

Write the following letters, one in each square, then cut out the squares:

| | | |
|---|---|---|
| 1. ch | 5. cr | 9. sn |
| 2. q | 6. tr | 10. sm |
| 3. br | 7. th | 11. wh |
| 4. v | 8. gr | 12. ph |

## How to play

Shuffle all the letter cards and place them face down in a pile on the table.

The first player takes the top card and sets the timer for two minutes.

The first player then says as many words as they can think of that start with the letter or letters they picked.

They stop speaking when the timer bleeps.

So if the player picked **ch** they might say:

**ch**urch

**ch**in

**ch**air

**ch**est

The player gets one point for each correct word.

Player two then picks up the next card and repeats what player one did.

Each player does this in turn until all the cards have been used.

The winner is the person who scores the most points overall.

If you are not sure about a word you can check with an adult, look it up on the internet or ask Alexa/Siri.

If it takes you time to think of words you could set the timer for five minutes. If the players are all very quick you could set it for 30 seconds. It's up to you.

If you want to play again shuffle the cards and start again. If you get the same letters try to think of different words each time.

You can add in your own letter or letter combinations.

**Ph** words are really sneaky; **ph** sounds like **f** and includes **photo** and **pharaoh** (king of Egypt). You could look up some **ph** words or swap **ph** for another letter.

When I was in school, I was told by a teacher to put a full stop or a comma down every time I would take a breath.

The problem with this is that I can talk for a really long time without taking a breath.

This made my sentences very long, with no commas!

This activity will help shorten your sentences, if you are like me.

## ▶ SING A SONG OF SENTENCES

*For two to four players.*

### You will *need*

- *a page of writing with full stops and commas taken out — you could ask a teacher or parent for this*

- *an answer page with full stops and commas still in*

- *scissors*

- *a pencil.*

I have included an example page you could use on page 70.

## How to play

You might like to ask an adult for help setting up this activity.

Take the page with the missing full stops and commas and cut it up into paragraphs (blocks of writing).

Number each paragraph on the back.

The first player picks a number and finds the paragraph with that number on the back.

The player then sings the words in their paragraph, adding commas and full stops when they need to breathe.

Short breaths will probably be commas and long breaths will probably be full stops.

Players can sing the words to any tune they like.

Remember that some full stops could be question marks.

Some full stops could be exclamation marks if

the sentence is very important or dramatic. For instance:

Where are we?

Watch out!

Check the answers against the answer page after each player has taken their turn.

Points can be given for full stops, commas, question marks and exclamation marks put in the right place. Points can also be scored for using the right punctuation mark.

Points can also be given for singing talent. If you can't agree on singing talent you could have a vote.

Possible score guide for singing talent:

1–3 points: could be better

4–6 points: mostly okay

7–9 points: good

10–12 points: very good

13–15 points: great.

*Example page without commas and full stops and other punctuation:*

## Monday 1st March

*St Davids Day*

*I live in Wales so we celebrate this David dude who has been well dead for ages but was important to Wales or something*

*What it means for me is I have to go to school looking like an idiot*

*When we were young we all had to dress up proper Welsh and get our photo taken as a class*

*Now I just have to have a leak pinned to my jumper*

*Still well embarrassing and someone shouted Oh look Cal the vegetable is wearing a vegetable when I walked into class*

*I didnt see who said it so I made out like I didnt hear it*

*(Taken from Diary of a Dyslexic School Kid)*

Example page with commas and full stops and other punctuation:

---

## Monday 1st March

St David's Day

I live in Wales, so we celebrate this David dude who has been well dead for ages but was important to Wales or something.

What it means for me is I have to go to school looking like an idiot.

When we were young, we all had to dress up proper Welsh and get our photo taken as a class.

Now I just have to have a leek pinned to my jumper.

Still well embarrassing and someone shouted, 'Oh look! Cal the vegetable is wearing a vegetable,' when I walked into class.

I didn't see who said it, so I made out like I didn't hear it.

(Taken from *Diary of a Dyslexic School Kid*)

---

*The main character, Cal, is dyslexic so there is some punctuation in the original, but I have given him some extra help here.*

# ▶ THE SPELLING BUMBLE BEE

For two or more players plus one judge.

## You will need

- card

- *scissors*

- *pens or pencils*

- *a timer (optional)*

- *a way to check spelling or example word cards.*

## How to play

Draw an insect on the same number of cards as there are players. For example, if there are four players draw on four cards.

Make sure that one card has a picture of a bumble bee on it.

Put the cards face down on the table.

Each player then chooses a card and turns it over to see the picture.

The player who picked the card with the bumble bee on will be asked to spell a word chosen by another player.

The judge needs to be able to check the spelling of the word chosen.

*The judge could use the internet, an electronic spell check or the example cards included below.*

*Each time the player with the bumble bee gets a letter correct the judge will say 'buzz'.*

*Players get one point for every buzz they get.*

*The winner is the person with the most points at the end of the game.*

*You could set a timer for an agreed number of minutes to indicate when the game finishes or finish the game when all players have had at least one turn at being the spelling bee.*

*Example spelling bee cards:*

| February | tomorrow | possess | government |
|----------|----------|---------|------------|
| kayak | friend | learn | ancient |
| tragedy | schedule | phrase | succeed |
| square | peppers | guitar | orphan |

# CHAPTER 7

# Ninja Story

Dyslexic learners are good at sounding out words. Often words will be read and spelt how they sound unless the letters get jumbled up like a jigsaw that doesn't fit.

The hard thing about using sounds to make up words is that there are lots of times when this does not work in English.

I worked with someone aged 8 who was finding it hard to read words that could not be sounded out.

Words like **tin** t-i-n were no problem, but even short words like **so** were hard as the o̱ was read as a short vowel (o̱, as in o̱ctopus), instead of a long vowel (o̱, as in o̱val).

The book he was given to read by school did not fit his age or interests, but books which did had higher reading levels.

As a result I wrote him his own story.

Some words in the story can be sounded out, like **Ninja**. Words that can't have been written correctly, but the sound version is in brackets.

You can start by reading the bits in brackets so you can read it on your own and then start to remember how the real word looks.

We drew pictures for doing words like **running**.

Parents, family friends or grandparents could make their own stories.

You could tell them what you want the story to be about: fairies, unicorns or dragons maybe.

'This story helped me learn the proper way to spell the word "said". Having the sounds in brackets made it easier to read on my own.' (Morgan, dyslexic learner)

# Ninja Sam

(<u>ow</u> = hurt sound)

# 1.

Ninja Sam did not know
(nO) h<u>ow</u> to read (reed).

So (sO) Ninja Sam
was (woz) sad.

## 2.

Ninja told (tOld) his dad.

His dad was (woz)
busy (bizee).

# 3.

Ninja told (tOld) his mum.

His mum was (woz) busy (bizee).

# 4.

Ninja told (tOld) his
friend (frend).

His friend (frend) was (woz)
busy (bizee) doing (doo
ing) fun things (fingz).

# 5.

Lots of (ov) people (pee pul) can read (reed).

But I don't (dOnt) know (nO) h<u>ow</u> said (sed) Ninja.

# 6.

Ninja was (woz) good (gud) at:

running

jumping

hiding

swimming

# 7.

But Ninja wanted (wont ed) to read (reed).

# 8.

Ninja told (tOld) a teacher (tee chur) and she said (sed) she would (wud) help.

## 9.

So (sO) Ninja read (red) and read (red) and read (red) and the teacher (tee chur) helped him.

# 10.

N<u>ow</u> Ninja can read (reed) a good (gud) story (stor ee).

# CHAPTER 8

# Does It Add Up?

Some dyslexics find maths hard because problems such as those about travel times on a bus compared with a train and a car are very wordy.

It can be tricky to know what sum you are meant to do.

Some dyslexics can also have dyscalculia (difficulty understanding numbers), and this can make maths a real challenge.

An important part of maths is learning times tables.

This can be a real struggle if your memory isn't great.

The next game is a fun way to practise multiplication.

#  THE MULTIPLY MATRIX GAME

*For two players.*

## You will need

- a sheet of A4 card

- a ruler

- a pencil

- a pen

- a die

- a playing piece (button/bottle top/small pebble).

## How to play

Using the ruler and pencil, draw 24 boxes on your sheet of card.

*Using a pen, write a number between 1 and 10 in each box in a random pattern. You can put your own numbers in the table — just try not to have too many repeats.*

*My example is on the next page. You can use this pattern to start with if you like.*

| | | | |
|---|---|---|---|
| 1 | 2 | 3 | 4 |
| 10 | 9 | 8 | 7 |
| 6 | 7 | 8 | 9 |
| 1 | 2 | 4 | 3 |
| 5 | 4 | 6 | 5 |
| 6 | 3 | 7 | 10 |

The first player starts at the top left-hand corner. They roll the die and move their counter that number of squares, moving from left to right along each row.

For example, if they roll five they land on a square that has the number **10** on it. They then multiply this number by the number on the square directly below, in this case **6**.

If their answer is correct (60) they move to the square below (6) taking them further on the board.

If their answer is incorrect they stay where they are (10) until their next go when they can try again.

The second player then roles the die and moves that number of squares.

Whichever number they land on they multiply it by the number directly below, and if the answer is right they move onto the square below.

The winner is the first player to reach the end of the board.

You can play as many times as you want.

# ▶ BLAST OFF GAME

For two to four players.

## You will *need*

- an old Scrabble™ board or large piece of card with squares drawn on (15x15) and a star drawn or a star sticker in the centre box

- counters/playing pieces

- *sticky notes*

- *pens*

- *paper*

- *a die*

- *a ruler*

- *a tape measure*

- *question cards with answers on the back (see the examples on page 144).*

## How to play

*Write the following:*

*Astronaut training*

*Building your rocket*

*Flight*

*Research*

*on four sticky notes and stick them in each corner of the Scrabble™/homemade board.*

Place questions that relate to each topic on the correct sticky note.

For example:

- 'Astronaut training' practical task questions such as: Count backwards from 100 whilst doing star jumps.

- 'Building your rocket' includes area and perimeter questions such as: The viewing window is a rectangle 6cm by 15cm. What is the perimeter of the window?

- 'Flight' includes any travel-related questions such as: Travelling at a speed of 90mph for 10 hours each day, how many days will it take to travel 63000 miles?

- 'Research' includes measurements, fractions and percentage questions such as: An asteroid weighing 210kg contains 70kg of carbon. What fraction of the asteroid is made up of carbon?

Select a square on the edge of the board to start from.

Player one rolls the die and moves the number of places shown on the die.

Once a player reaches the first sticky note, they select the top question and answer it.

If the answer is correct they collect the card.

If the answer is incorrect they place the card at the bottom of the pile.

The next player/s then take their turn.

When it is the next turn of player one they answer the next question down.

Once a player has collected four cards, one from each sticky note, they make their way to the square in the centre of the board and shout 'Blast off'.

The first player to do this is the winner.

#  NUMBER TAG

*For three or more players.*

## You will need

- a notepad and pen to keep score

- a timer or stopwatch.

## How to play

Decide if you want to play the multiplication or addition version of the game.

Each player picks a number between 2 and 10.

Player one (this could be the youngest player) starts.

Set the timer for five minutes.

Player one is 'it'.

They call out their number and then tag another player.

The player who is tagged must then either add player one's number and theirs (addition version) or multiply them (multiplication version).

For example, if player one picks number 4, they start by calling: 4.

Player one then tags another player.

If that tagged player picks number 6, they add the two numbers together and shout: 10.

If playing the multiplication version, the tagged player multiplies the two numbers and shouts: 24.

If the tagged player answers correctly then they tag another player.

The player that they tag must answer the new sum. For example, if the next player picked 3 they would answer either 6 plus 3 (addition version) or 6 times 3 (multiplication version).

If they answer incorrectly, then **they** must answer when they have tagged another player and have a new sum.

Ask someone to keep score, one point for every correct answer (the players can take this in turns, or an adult could help).

The game ends when either every player has been tagged at least once, or the five-minute timer goes off.

# CHAPTER 9

# For Parents and Guardians

If you are younger than sixteen and reading this – stop now!

This chapter is not for you.

There are no secrets in it; it is just dull, dull, dull!

It will be super boring for you.

So, I beg you, please skip to the next chapter, which is more fun.

Then, when you have finished this book, give it to mum or dad or whoever takes care of you (usually the person who gives you food) and ask them to read this chapter.

## Don't stress

If you have just found out that your child is dyslexic, or you think they might be, this does not mean that your child won't be able to achieve academically. They are highly likely to need support and to find a different approach to learning, one which suits them.

There are dyslexic scientists, politicians, writers, inventors and entrepreneurs amongst many other professions.

You will find dyslexic people in all walks of life.

Your child's brain works differently to those of non-dyslexics, but this should never hold them back or prevent them from fulfilling their aspirations and dreams.

## Dyslexia and online learning

I want to include this topic as online learning is becoming more prevalent in education, partly as a result of lockdowns due to Covid-19 (which I hope will be a thing of the past by the time this is published). It is also being increasingly used as a teaching tool by schools across the country.

Online learning can present a whole new set of challenges for a dyslexic learner.

Many dyslexic learners can find looking at words on a screen difficult and changing the background colour may help. Check toolbar options to change background screen colour.

As well as finding it hard to see words on a screen, dyslexic learners could also misunderstand the task being asked of them.

If this happens it would be useful to ask the school if there are times when a 'chat box' can be accessed either with the teacher or a learning support assistant (LSA) who could clarify exactly what the task involves.

Regular breaks will be important; even if your young person can watch TV or play computer games for hours on end, learning is different.

During breaks try to encourage tasks that directly appeal to the learner's preferred style. For example, if they learn best through movement, send them on a hunt through the house and garden (if you have one) to locate a clue that relates to the next task.

Visual and 'hands on' learners could be asked to sort pens or toy blocks, for example, into different colours. This activity has been shown to increase creative thinking in subsequent tasks.

To reinforce and embed their learning, musical learners could make up a song that sums up what they have just learnt in a task.

Some dyslexic learners are better suited to online learning as it can provide a quieter working environment and allow for more control over the learning, for example being able to decide when to take a break.

Useful online resources include:

- Twinkl (free downloadable worksheets/activities, etc. on a range of topics)

- BBC Bitesize (various ages and topics available) – Karate Cats (spelling and punctuation quiz) is my current favourite.

Some charities can provide access to laptops and printers – please check your local area for this.

# Mental health and wellbeing

It could be argued that a child's mental health and wellbeing are just as important as academic success, if not more so.

This can mean different things to different people. However, in the work I do the two key features covered by this are confidence and resilience.

Confidence is often very low when I start working with a young dyslexic.

The individual concerned may have been given the message that they are 'not good enough'. These days this may not come directly from teachers but may be more subtle.

For example, if Lucy finishes a piece of work well after everyone in her class, she may start to think she is slow or not as capable as her peers, even if no negative comments are made.

Praising the things Lucy excels in is a good place to start – her drawings or ability to work well in a team, for instance.

It is also important, especially with dyslexic learners, to praise effort rather than outcome.

For example, try saying 'I'm impressed how much time you spent on this project and how committed you were to the piece of work', rather than only giving praise if the learner achieves the top mark for their work.

It could take some time to build confidence. In my experience, reassuring the learner I work with that they are smart and capable but have been trying to learn in a way less suited to their brain has always proved helpful in building their confidence.

Resilience is a tougher one for me and something I am still working on in myself. For me resilience is about being able to pick myself up again when things go wrong.

You could try the following:

- meditation

- mindfulness

- tai chi/yoga

- gratitude lists

all of which are now accessible in some form for young people as well as adults.

One of the most helpful techniques for me personally is re-framing the internal monologue.

For instance, instead of thinking 'I can't do this', I try changing it to 'I haven't mastered this yet'. Instead of 'I got it all wrong', 'I made some mistakes, and I can learn from them'. This can be very useful but is not always easy to do. Sometimes I just need to take time out to do something I love before returning to the challenge at hand.

## A note about rewards

Rewards are very important in learning but are often forgotten about or overlooked.

A reward releases a happy chemical in our brain that we then associate with the experience, for example the completion of a task. This then becomes a strong motivation for the future.

As adults, when we finish something most of us have a real sense of achievement which makes us feel happy – an internal reward. However, we all benefit from external rewards.

The reward does not need to be big or expensive;

it could be stickers or smiley faces, or it could be extra time allotted to play a favourite game or watch television.

## Diagnosis

The rest of this chapter is an updated version of Chapter 9 in *Fun Games and Activities for Children with Dyslexia* to which this book is the sequel. Much of the following information has not changed since that book's publication in 2018 so remains largely unchanged here.

In terms of diagnosis and assessment, there are two different aspects to consider. These are: internal school tests and those carried out by educational psychologists (an Individual Education Plan, usually known as an IEP).

### School

Your child's school may do an internal assessment, which would normally identify those at risk of dyslexia or with dyslexic tendencies.

Schools use different tests. I am aware of at least

three different tests at schools within the same county.

If your child's dyslexia is severe, or they have additional learning requirements, the school may recommend, or refer you to, an educational psychologist for a full assessment.

Schools are able to provide a level of support without a report (IEP) written by an educational psychologist.

Support for dyslexic learners may include:

- extra time in exams

- coloured overlays (reading rulers)

- a reader in exams

- Read&Write Gold software

- C-PEN® ReaderPen™ (especially the ExamReader™ pen)

- a learning support assistant in the classroom.

When extra time in exams is required, an application is usually made by the school to the examining board to allow more time for the learner.

The application may take time, so the sooner this is identified and requested, the better.

Coloured overlays (reading rulers) are available from Crossbow Education (see Resources) and can assist reading in dyslexic learners, especially for those with the associated condition Irlen Syndrome. Coloured overlays do not work for all dyslexics and current scientific research is inconclusive. However, in practice these overlays can be a useful tool but should not be used in isolation. I would also always recommend an assessment by an optician if any visual issues are presented. A very well-known high street opticians has been assessing the benefit of coloured lenses and recommending where appropriate for a number of years.

A reader in exams is usually a member of the learning support team who can read exam questions out loud to the learner.

Read&Write Gold is software aimed at assisting dyslexic learners (see Resources). Key features include a toolbar allowing the learner to play text aloud through headphones, links to various dictionaries and an ability to save web addresses for research purposes.

A C-PEN® ReaderPen™ (see Resources) can be used to scan text, from any source, and can read text aloud through headphones.

As the C-PEN® has an attached camera, as opposed to a laser, it can read almost any text.

The first time I used the C-PEN®, I really put it to the test, using it on photocopies, underlining and highlighted paragraphs (that was a fun day!).

It also has a dictionary function. If you scan a word, the definition appears underneath on the LED screen.

The C-PEN® is easy technology to use (it really is Alais proof) and is great for independent study.

For schools, in particular, the ExamReader™ pen can be very useful. It has the same operational function as the C-PEN® ReaderPen™ described above but has been approved by exam boards. This means it could be used by a young person even if they have not been diagnosed with dyslexia, and the school doesn't need to apply for access arrangements for an individual to use it.

Alongside other qualifications it can be used for the GCSE English comprehension paper.

The company that produces the C-PEN® is also involved in a number of projects for dyslexic learners. A recent project, run in a number of schools, was called 'Drop Everything and Read' – DEAR – and promoted reading and support for reading.

Also available is a detective story designed to help young people practise their use of the C-PEN®; I am looking forward to reading it myself.

Scanmarkers are also available; they perform a similar basic function to the C-PEN® ReaderPen™. However, I have not used a Scanmarker myself, so am unable to give a detailed description. I have included a link in the Resources to someone using both and comparing the C-PEN® ReaderPen™ with the Scanmarker.

A learning support assistant in the classroom is an individual who can work with the learner, clarifying anything that hasn't been understood and advising and supporting where nedeed, based upon the individual learner's requirements.

All of the support listed above, except extra time in exams, is subject to the school your child attends having enough funding and resources to deliver any of these provisions.

## Individual Education Plans

It is a long time, over 20 years, since my own assessment was carried out by an educational psychologist.

I wanted more up-to-date information, so I spoke with the principal of the Helen Arkell Centre (see Resources) who, amongst other things, provide assessments (IEPs) where required.

The first point to make is that an IEP comes with a financial cost and, in isolation, may not be an effective solution.

Your local education authority may decide that any assistances highlighted in the report are recommendations and therefore do not have to be implemented.

Currently in the UK, dyslexia is the least likely learning difference to be able to access support despite reports (IEPs), and, sadly, an IEP offers no guarantee of support.

As with schools, much of the support available will be dependent upon resources and funding.

From my own assessment, I was lucky enough to be provided with all the technology, tools and support suggested in the report.

The only part I found challenging was being given a reading age. At the age of 19, and whilst undertaking a degree, I was given a reading age of nine.

This was very disheartening. It knocked my confidence, and I was all too aware that I would still be expected to read information at degree level.

This also seemed to me to be quite subjective. I have personally known readers of all ages to vary greatly in their abilities, so an age is not perhaps the most objective way of expressing this data.

In recent years there has been a move away from reading age and towards the use of a standard score more closely akin to how IQ is measured.

Making sure that the result and outcome are not seen as 'failure' for the young person concerned is obviously key.

I often compare it to athletics.

If you are running a 500-metre race but your starting block is 100 metres behind all the other runners, it will take you longer to 'catch up'.

We all have our starting blocks for learning in different places, but it is fairer if we are not judged as if we were all starting at the same point.

So, to return to the question about whether an individual is dyslexic, a parent who is dyslexic would now be seen as presenting a key 'at risk' factor.

Dyslexia can range from mild to severe and so may be picked up at different stages and may also require different strategies.

In my opinion, if a child finds reading and spelling challenging, typically writes some or all letters back to front and in the wrong order, finds traditional teaching methods ineffective, and yet is creative and appears bright and capable at things which don't involve reading and writing, it is worth asking the question about dyslexia as a possible explanation.

## So what can parents do?

If you think your child is dyslexic, as a parent or guardian you could liaise with the school. Ask about challenges that you could work on together at home.

Play word games together on a regular basis and explain any new words used.

Encourage reading for fun at home and read together whenever possible.

Possible complications:

- You are also dyslexic.

- You work long hours.

If either or both of these are the case then you could consider the following:

- Purchase some pre-made games (see Resources).

- Try adult literacy classes (many community education centres/colleges offer classes for free).

- Work at a level you are confident with.

- Get support from other family members and friends. You may have a family member or friend who really enjoys word games and is just waiting for an invitation to play them with you and your child.

- You can also find some interesting word games online.

- Purchase a C-PEN® ReaderPen™ (described in the school section of this chapter), as this can be used to scan text and read it aloud and also has a dictionary function. It can be very useful to use at home as well as in school. This excellent bit of kit can allow for independent learning and study. It also comes with free upgrades and a free 14-day trial for parents, which can be found online (see Resources).

- If your child hasn't already done it, ask them the questions from Chapter 2 to find out how they learn best, and then look at the relevant chapter (e.g. 'I Like to Move It') for more ideas.

# CHAPTER 10

# My 'Yoda' Bit (Wise Words)

## Have fun!

We might all have different ideas about what games or activities are fun.

Fun can also change over time.

I used to love water pistol games as a child, but as an adult getting wet deliberately seems less fun.

You know yourself and what you find fun better than anyone else.

We learn best when we are having fun.

I hope you have found the games in this book fun and that they have helped your learning too.

# Be brave!

Sometimes it is scary to try new things.

What if it doesn't work out?

What if I mess it up?

I might end up looking like a fool!

It is normal to have these fears and worries, but trying new things is important.

If you never try anything new you will only know what you know now.

I went horse riding again a couple of years ago.

I stopped learning when I was young because the horse went faster than I was ready to go.

Then the same thing happened on a trip abroad some years later.

This time I told the instructors about what had happened, and they were very supportive.

They explained that I was signalling the horse to slow down and stop with the reins, but because my heels were raised I was also telling the horse to go faster.

This new learning has helped my confidence.

They also explained that although I had been on a horse that 'ran away with me', because I managed to stay on until an instructor rescued me I had not failed at riding a horse but actually succeeded in staying on.

I also tried paddle boarding for the first time last year.

I didn't get to a point where I could stand up on the board.

However, I really enjoyed the session and learnt how to steer the board with my oar.

When we are doing new things we may not learn what we set out to, but we always learn something.

## Be kind to yourself!

When you find something challenging, be kind to yourself.

It may take you a long time to do a task.

If you think it will take time be patient with yourself.

Ask for help if you need it.

I still ask people to help me with filling in forms and computer-related stuff.

Some people will love the stuff you find hard – give them a chance to shine.

You can shine at what you do best!

# Thank you!

Finally, I would like to say a big thank you for reading this book.

I hope you have enjoyed the games and that it gives you ideas for your own games too.

I worked with a student not long ago.

They told me, 'If I didn't have this brain thing, I could read everything'.

I had a think about this.

Then I said, 'But that just makes you even more amazing'.

They asked me what I meant.

I said, 'If you find something very hard the fact that you can do it at all makes you amazing'.

So please remember: if you have read any of this book or played the games and you find reading and spelling hard you are amazing!

In fact you are a superstar – be proud!

# Resources

## Helpful websites

www.bdadyslexia.org.uk – British Dyslexia Association

www.helenarkell.org.uk – Provides assessments and advice, etc. for dyslexics

www.dyslexia-london.com – Educational psychologist: provides assessments for young people and adults

www.dyslexicinsight.com – Specialist tuition for dyslexic learners (Australia)

www.twinkl.co.uk – Variety of learning resources

www.spellzone.com – Spelling: useful for word pattern lists, e.g. words ending 'cian', etc.

www.wordhippo.com – Thesaurus and definitions: useful for new words and meanings

www.youtube.com/watch?v=ylPxPU42XSI – Connect Pen vs. Scanmarker Air | Digital Highlighter Comparison

www.bbc.co.uk/bitesize/topics/zvwwxnb/articles/zc773k7 – Commas use

www.twinkl.co.uk/resource/us-t-2549043-commas-punctuation-display-poster – Commas poster

## Stuff to buy

www.cpen.com – C-PEN® ReaderPen™

www.crossboweducation.com – Reading rulers (variety of colours) and educational games (word puzzles, etc.)

www.texthelp.com – Read&Write Gold software

www.uberkids.com – Sight Words Bingo

www.amazon.co.uk – First Words (Brighter Child Flashcards) Cards

## Books

Finlay, M. (2015) *Everyday English for Grown-Ups*. London: Michael O'Mara Books Ltd.

Gardner, H. (2006) *Multiple Intelligences*. New York: Basic Books.

Hornigold, J. (2021) *Awesome Games and Activities for Kids with Numeracy Difficulties*. London and Philadelphia: Jessica Kingsley Publishers.

Parkinson, J. (2007) *I Before E (Except After C)*. London: Michael O'Mara Books Ltd.

Winton, A. (2015) *The Self-Help Guide for Teens with Dyslexia*. London and Philadelphia: Jessica Kingsley Publishers.

Winton, A. (2018) *Fun Games and Activities for Children with Dyslexia*. London and Philadelphia: Jessica Kingsley Publishers.

# Example Templates

# Star game

| The past tense of do is: | The past tense of teach is: | The past tense of get is: | The past tense of bring is: |
|---|---|---|---|
| 1. Does | 1. Teached | 1. Got | 1. Bringed |
| 2. Did | 2. Teacher | 2. Goten | 2. Brung |
| 3. Doesn't | 3. Taught | 3. Getted | 3. Brought |
| **The past tense of run is:** | **The past tense of go is:** | **Read the following words:** | **Read the following words:** |
| 1. Ran | 1. Goed | 1. Answer | 1. Mother |
| 2. Runed | 2. Went | 2. Only | 2. Made |
| 3. Running | 3. Gone | 3. Once | 3. Many |
| | | | 4. More |

Read the following words:
1. Father
2. Find
3. First
4. Fast

Read the following words:
1. With
2. Gnome
3. Sword

Read the following words:
1. This
2. That
3. These
4. Those

Read the following words:
1. Balloon
2. Elephant
3. Restaurant

Read the following words:
1. Skill
2. Ball
3. One

Read the following words:
1. Chick
2. Window
3. Bread

Read the following words:
1. Tall
2. Hook
3. Make

Read the following words:
1. Wall
2. Cook
3. When

| Which is the correct spelling? | Which is the correct spelling? | Which is the correct spelling? |
|---|---|---|
| 1. Jumpd | 1. Light | 1. Feeld |
| 2. Jumped | 2. Lite | 2. Field |
| 3. Jumpt | 3. Liet | 3. Feild |

| Which is the correct spelling? | Which is the correct spelling? | Which is the correct spelling? |
|---|---|---|
| 1. Shud | | 1. Majic |
| 2. Shood | | 2. Magic |
| 3. Should | | 3. Majek |

| Which is the correct spelling? | Which is the correct spelling? | Which is the correct spelling? |
|---|---|---|
| 1. Norty | 1. Head | 1. Does |
| 2. Nortee | 2. Hed | 2. Dus |
| 3. Naughty | 3. Hede | 3. Duse |

| Mystery spelling Another player will ask you to spell a word. | Mystery spelling Another player will ask you to spell a word. | Which is the correct spelling?<br><br>1. White<br><br>2. Wite<br><br>3. Wyte | Which is the correct spelling?<br><br>1. Cort<br><br>2. Coght<br><br>3. Caught |
|---|---|---|---|
| What is the past tense of think?<br><br>1. Thunk<br><br>2. Thinked<br><br>3. Thought | What is the past tense of find?<br><br>1. Found<br><br>2. Finded<br><br>3. Finds | What is the past tense of sleep?<br><br>1. Sleeped<br><br>2. Slept<br><br>3. Sleeps | What is the past tense of speak?<br><br>1. Speaked<br><br>2. Spoke<br><br>3. Speach |

# Star game example answer sheet

*Past tense cards:*

Do = 2. Did                   Bring = 3. Brought

Teach = 3. Taught             Run = 1. Ran

Get = 1. Got                  Go = 2. Went

*Spelling cards:*

2. Jumped                     1. Head

1. Light                      1. Does

3. Should                     2. Magic

2. Field                      1. White

3. Naughty                    3. Caught

*More past tense cards:*

Think = 3. Thought            Sleep = 2. Slept

Find = 1. Found               Speak = 2. Spoke

✴

# Verb super score

## Go
Power: 2
Syllables: 1
Spelling skill: 1
Alphabetical order: 7

## Run
Power: 5
Syllables: 1
Spelling skill: 1
Alphabetical order: 18

## Sprint
Power: 9
Syllables: 1
Spelling skill: 3
Alphabetical order: 19

## Eat
Power: 2
Syllables: 1
Spelling skill: 3
Alphabetical order: 5

## Consume
Power: 6
Syllables: 2
Spelling skill: 6
Alphabetical order: 3

## Devour
Power: 9
Syllables: 2
Spelling skill: 7
Alphabetical order: 4

## Ask
Power: 2
Syllables: 1
Spelling skill: 3
Alphabetical order: 1

## Question
Power: 6
Syllables: 2
Spelling skill: 7
Alphabetical order: 17

## Demand
Power: 8
Syllables: 2
Spelling skill: 5
Alphabetical order: 4

## Do
Power: 1
Syllables: 1
Spelling skill: 1
Alphabetical order: 4

## Complete
Power: 9
Syllables: 2
Spelling skill: 5
Alphabetical order: 3

## Say
Power: 2
Syllables: 1
Spelling skill: 2
Alphabetical order: 19

**Bellow**
Power: 10
Syllables: 2
Spelling skill: 6
Alphabetical order: 2

**Walk**
Power: 3
Syllables: 1
Spelling skill: 2
Alphabetical order: 23

**Pace**
Power: 9
Syllables: 1
Spelling skill: 4
Alphabetical order: 16

**Jump**
Power: 2
Syllables: 1
Spelling skill: 2
Alphabetical order: 10

**Spring**
Power: 9
Syllables: 1
Spelling skill: 5
Alphabetical order: 19

**Move**
Power: 2
Syllables: 1
Spelling skill: 2
Alphabetical order: 13

### Climb
Power: 5
Syllables: 1
Spelling skill: 7
Alphabetical order: 3

### Hurl
Power: 10
Syllables: 1
Spelling skill: 5
Alphabetical order: 8

### Scramble
Power: 10
Syllables: 2
Spelling skill: 8
Alphabetical order: 19

### Get
Power: 2
Syllables: 1
Spelling skill: 2
Alphabetical order: 7

### Throw
Power: 4
Syllables: 1
Spelling skill: 6
Alphabetical order: 20

### Receive
Power: 9
Syllables: 2
Spelling skill: 9
Alphabetical order: 18

## Fly

Power: 3

Syllables: 1

Spelling skill: 3

Alphabetical order: 6

## Glide

Power: 7

Syllables: 1

Spelling skill: 4

Alphabetical order: 7

## Soar

Power: 10

Syllables: 1

Spelling skill: 4

Alphabetical order: 19

# Verb super score template

|  |  |  |
|--|--|--|
|  |  |  |
|  |  |  |
|  |  |  |

# Shakespeare pairs cards

| hath | shouldst | cometh | hither |
|------|----------|--------|--------|
| art  | wilt     | saith  | shalt  |
| thou | doth     | thy    | nay    |

| | | |
|---|---|---|
| here | comes | should | has |
| shall | says | will | are |
| no | your | do/does | you |

# Answers to Shakespeare pairs

hath = has

shouldst = should

cometh = comes

hither = here

art = are

wilt = will

saith = says

shalt = shall

thou = you

doth = do/does

thy = your

nay = no

# Blast off game example questions

The viewing window is a rectangle 6cm by 15cm. What is the perimeter of the window?

1. 44cm
2. 48cm
3. 42cm

There will be three astronauts, and each is given a weight allowance of 4.38kg. What is the total allowance?

1. 13.85kg
2. 13.02kg
3. 13.14kg

The console length is 147mm. What is this in cm?

1. 147cm
2. 14.7cm
3. 1.47cm

A floor panel is a rectangle 10cm by 7cm. What is the area of the panel?

1. $70cm^2$
2. $170cm^2$
3. $700cm^2$

Count backwards from 100 whilst doing star jumps.

Draw a scale model of the latest space rover (Curiosity) which is 3m long, 2.8m wide and 2.1m high. Wheels are 50.8cm diameter. Scale: 3cm = 1m.

Count up to 1 minute 20 seconds in your head. Shout 'done' when you have finished. Ask someone to set a timer/stopwatch to check this.

Use a tape measure to measure the length of your leg (from your hip to the base of your foot). Divide this number by the width of your hand. What is your answer?

An asteroid weighing 210kg contains 70kg of carbon. What fraction of the asteroid is made up of carbon?

1. One fifth

2. One quarter

3. One third

---

You are measuring 90ml of liquid found on the moon's surface. If 10% is sodium how much sodium is present?

1. 10ml

2. 9ml

3. 18ml

---

On Mars every three out of six days has a temperature of over 100°C. What percentage of the time will the temperature be above 100°C?

1. 30%

2. 50%

3. 60%

---

The space rover travels 32 metres per hour. How many metres will it cover in 14 hours?

1. 448 metres

2. 560 metres

3. 320 metres

Travelling at a speed of 90mph for 10 hours each day, how many days will it take to travel 63000miles?

1. 70 days

2. 700 days

3. 35 days

---

On launch the rocket needs to be attached to the base at a right angle. How many degrees is this?

1. 180°

2. 120°

3. 90°

---

You are plotting a triangulated course. On the base line both angles are 70°. What is the angle of the triangle you are heading towards?

1. 40°

2. 60°

3. 70°

---

If the Earth is 94.51 million miles from the sun and Mars is 155.24 million miles from the sun, round up or down to find the approximate distance between them.

1. 60 million miles

2. 61 million miles

3. 63 million miles

# Blast off game example answers

| | | |
|---|---|---|
| 1. 44cm<br>2. 48cm<br>**3. 42cm** | 1. 147cm<br>**2. 14.7cm**<br>3. 1.47cm | 1. **70cm$^2$**<br>2. 170cm$^2$<br>3. 700cm$^2$ |
| Length: 9cm<br>Width: 8.4 cm<br>Height: 6.3cm<br>Wheels: 1.524cm diameter. | Did you count in time with the stop watch? | Ask another player to check your measurements and answer. |
| Star jumps, counting backwards. How many did you do? Decide as a group how many you need to do to win the card. | | |

| | | | |
|---|---|---|---|
| 1. **448 metres**<br>2. 560 metres<br>3. 320 metres | 1. 30%<br>2. **50%**<br>3. 60% | 1. 10ml<br>2. **9ml**<br>3. 18ml | 1. One fifth<br>2. One quarter<br>3. **One third** |
| 1. **60 million miles**<br>2. 61 million miles<br>3. 63 million miles | 1. **40°**<br>2. 60°<br>3. 70° | 1. 180°<br>2. 120°<br>3. **90°** | 1. **70 days**<br>2. 700 days<br>3. 35 days |

# Index

**Fun Games and Activities for Children with Dyslexia**
**How to Learn Smarter with a Dyslexic Brain**
*Alais Winton*
*Illustrated by Joe Salerno*
ISBN 978 1 78592 292 3
eISBN 978 1 78450 596 7

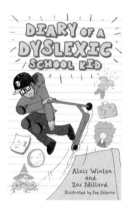

**Diary of a Dyslexic School Kid**
*Alais Winton and Zac Millard*
*Illustrated by Joe Salerno*
ISBN 978 1 78592 442 2
eISBN 978 1 78450 814 2

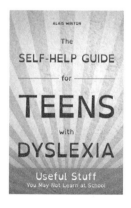

**The Self-Help Guide for Teens with Dyslexia**
**Useful Stuff You May Not Learn at School**
*Alais Winton*
ISBN 978 1 84905 649 6
eISBN 978 1 78450 144 0

*of related interest*

**Dyslexia is My Superpower (Most of the Time)**
Margaret Rooke
*Forewords by Catherine Drennan and Loyle Carner*
ISBN 978 1 78592 299 2
eISBN 978 1 78450 606 3

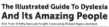

**The Illustrated Guide To Dyslexia and Its Amazing People**
*Kate Power and Kathy Iwanczak Forsyth*
*Foreword by Richard Rogers, Architect*
ISBN 978 1 78592 330 2
eISBN 978 1 78450 647 6

**Awesome Games and Activities for Kids with Numeracy Difficulties**
**How to Feel Smart and In Control about Doing Mathematics with a Neurodiverse Brain**
Judy Hornigold
*Illustrated by Joe Salerno*
ISBN 978 1 78775 563 5
eISBN 978 1 78775 564 2